MW00574520

Contents

FJH2021

First Light

Since my youngest son was born, he has awakened me early—and frequently—allowing me to see a lot of sunrises!
There's something magical about those moments when darkness gradually gives way to the first light of the day.

Kevin Olson

My Kind of Music

BOOK 4

Intermediate

Kevin Olson

Note from the Composer

Isn't it great when you find a piece of music that perfectly captures who you are, what you like, and how you think? Maybe you really like the title, or the melody stays in your head all day, or maybe it's just simply a blast to play! When you feel that special connection with a musical work, you want to play it and hear it over and over again. I created these compositions with you in mind, hoping that some of them would connect with you in that exciting way. Best wishes in your discovery of pieces about which you could exclaim, "Hey! That's my kind of music!"

Kevin R. Olson

Kevin Olson

6

The Big Easy Blues

Like most Americans, I was shocked to see the devastation left in New Orleans in the wake of Hurricane Katrina in 2005. But I have also been inspired to see the resilience of the "Big Easy," as New Orleans is called, rebound as volunteers from all over the world combined efforts to rebuild the great city of jazz. This piece celebrates the spirit of optimism that shines in the music of New Orleans.

Quickly; with attitude! (♩ = 144)
straight eighths; no swing

8

On the Wings of Pegasus

In Greek mythology, Pegasus was a winged horse who accompanied Perseus on many adventures. Like other immortal gods, Pegasus lives on as a constellation that can be seen in the Northern Hemisphere during the Fall. At the end of the piece, try to capture the thundering hooves softly disappearing across the horizon.

12

FJH2021

Gettysburg

The fields of Gettysburg in southern Pennsylvania have been immortalized as a turning point in the Civil War. In four days of intense fighting, Union soldiers turned back an aggressive Confederate attack, gaining morale and momentum that would eventually lead to Confederate surrender two years later. Try to capture the solemn pride and courage of the Americans on both sides of the war who lost their lives in Gettysburg.

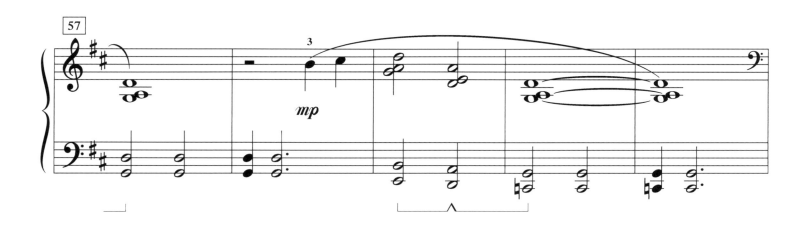

fading away and slowing down

FJH2021

Ghostdance

Don't get scared now—all the minor tonality and chromaticism in the world can't hurt you!
Practice slowly at first, so that when the ghosts begin to dance you can keep up.

Toccata in Twilight

*My favorite time of the day is right after the sun sets. The colors in the sky seem to change every few seconds,
giving interesting hues to the world below. This piece tries to capture those ever-changing colors before they
disappear into darkness at the end.*

Mysteriously; with forward motion (♩ = 176)

Catching Fireflies

Growing up in Utah, I'd heard of fireflies but I'd never seen any. Summer in the Midwest means our front lawn lights up every night with the glow of the lampyridae, or as they're more commonly known, "fireflies." Bring out the top notes in the melody line that are marked tenuto.

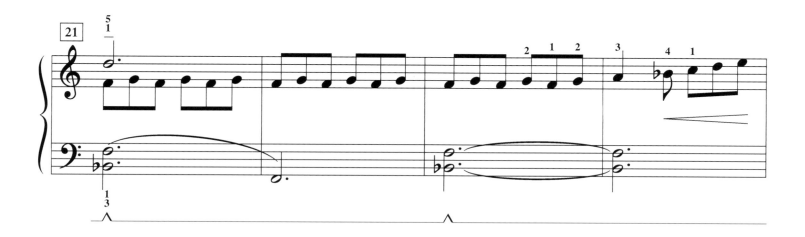

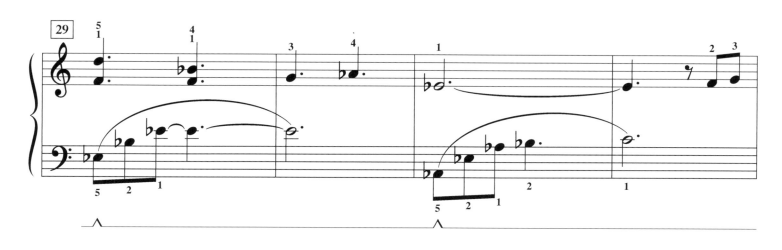

FJH2021

L.H. over

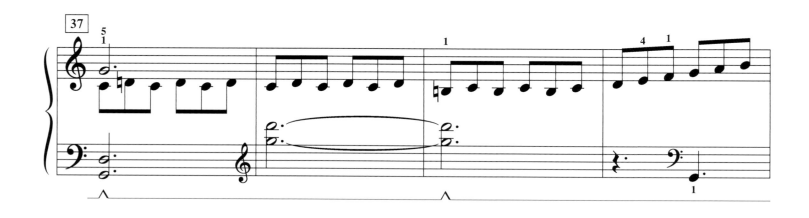

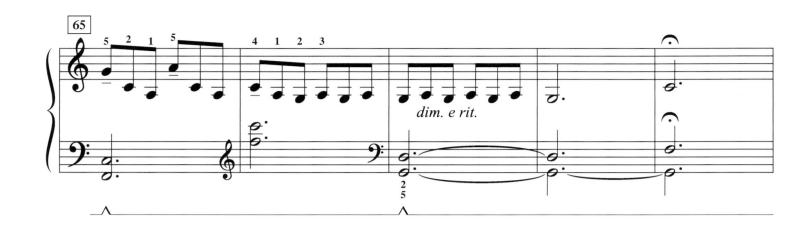

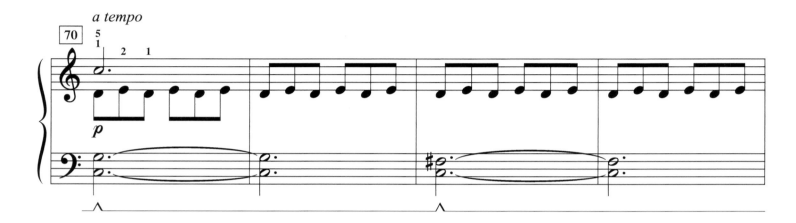

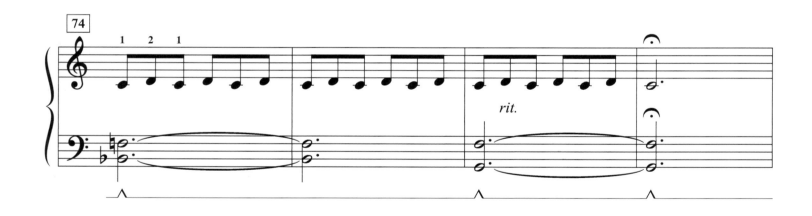

* *gradually lift pedal*

FJH2021